D0529737

Note to Parents and Teachers

The SCIENCE STARTERS series introduces key science vocabulary and concepts to young children while encouraging them to discover and understand the world around them. The series works as a set of graded readers in three levels.

LEVEL 3: READ ALONE
These books can be read alone or as part of guided or group reading. Each book has three sections:

• Information pages that introduce key concepts. Key words appear in bold for easy recognition on pages where the related science concepts are explained.
• A lively story that recalls this vocabulary and encourages children to use these words when they talk and write.
• A quiz asks children to look back and recall what they have read.

ANTS to WHALES looks at THE ANIMAL KINGDOM. Below are some answers and activities related to the questions on the information spreads that parents, carers, and teachers can use to discuss and develop further ideas and concepts:

p. 4 *Collect pictures of animals. Sort them into these six main groups.* You could introduce other groups such as crustaceans and mollusks.

p. 6 *Why do you think backbones are not just one long bone?* Get children to explore different parts of their skeleton, e.g. to look for biggest/smallest bone. You could expand this by talking about how muscles and bones work together to help animals move.

p. 9 *Can you think of animals that swim, slither, creep, crawl, or scuttle?* Encourage children to explore and expand their vocabulary. You could play a game where they try to match words for movement with particular animals or enact the movements.

p. 11 *What flying insects visit flowers?* You could mention how animals and plants live and work together. Plants produce sweet nectar/fruits/nuts so that animals will help them to pollinate/scatter their seeds.

p. 13 *What other than a car or shark has a long, smooth shape?* Ask children to link animals and machines e.g. bird and airplane, fish and submarine. You could also mention the smooth body suits that some athletes wear to help them swim or run faster.

p. 17 *What happens to your old skin?* It flakes off. You could also expand by comparing with changes in other animals as they grow, e.g. frog, butterfly, grasshopper.

p. 19 *Does it (a feather) feel light or heavy?* You could also mention that feathers keep birds warm and dry and that feathers need care, e.g. birds oil and wash their feathers.

ADVISORY TEAM

Educational Consultant
Andrea Bright—Science Coordinator, Trafalgar Junior School

Literacy Consultant
Jackie Holderness—former Senior Lecturer in Primary Education, Westminster Institute, Oxford Brookes University

Series Consultants
Anne Fussell—Early Years Teacher and University Tutor, Westminster Institute, Oxford Brookes University

David Fussell—C.Chem., FRSC

CONTENTS

© Aladdin Books Ltd 2006

Designed and produced by
Aladdin Books Ltd

First published in
the United States in 2006 by
Stargazer Books
c/o The Creative Company
123 South Broad Street
P.O. Box 227, Mankato,
Minnesota 56002

Printed in Malaysia
All rights reserved

Editor: Jim Pipe
Design: Flick, Book Design
and Graphics

Thanks to:
• The pupils of Trafalgar Infants
School for appearing as models in this
book, and to Lynne Thompson for
helping to organize the photoshoots.
• The pupils and teachers of
Trafalgar Junior School and St.
Nicholas C.E. Infant School for
testing the sample books.

Library of Congress Cataloging-in-Publication Data

Hewitt, Sally, 1949-
    Animal kingdom / by Sally Hewitt.
    p. cm. -- (Science starters. Level 3)
    ISBN 1-59604-009-2
    1. Animals--Juvenile literature.
    I. Title. II. Series

QL49.H565 2005
590--dc22
                        2005046459

Photocredits:
*l-left, r-right, b-bottom, t-top,
c-center, m-middle*
Cover tl & tr, 2bl, 7tr, 18b, 19tr,
23mr, 27t, 31bl — Stockbyte.
Cover tm, 15b, 16tr — Photodisc.
Cover main, 2ml, 5tc, 9m, 12t,
13t, 13m, 18tr, 20tr, 20b, 22b —
Corbis. 2tl, 3, 8b, 10b, 14b, 16mr,
29ml, 29br, 31ml, 31ml — Digital
Vision. 4, 31tr — Comstock. 5tl,
5tr, 5bl, 5br, 9b, 15m, 17tl, 21mr,
24mr, 25b, 26br — Ingram
Publishing. 5bc, 7br, 12b, 21t,
23br, 30mr, 31bc, 31bl — John
Foxx Images. 6t, 17b, 25t —
Select Pictures. 6b — PBD. 7m,
16b, 17br, 30tl — Flick Smith. 8t,
10t, 10b — Otto Rogge
Photography. 9t, 21bl — NOAA.
10-11, 26ml — USDA. 13b — US
Navy. 14t, 19b, 24b, 26tr, 27b —
Jim Pipe. 15t, 23tr — Corel. 19tl,
28t, 29tr — US Fish & Wildlife
Service. 22tr — Brand X Pictures.
28br — David Jones

ANIMAL KINGDOM

Ants to Whales

by Sally Hewitt

Stargazer Books

ANIMAL KINGDOM

Animals can be found everywhere on Earth, from the tops of mountains to deep under the sea.

There are about two million different kinds of animal. They all belong to the **animal kingdom**.

You are a kind of animal called a human.

Human

Dog

Collect pictures of animals. Then sort them into the groups on page 5.

What group do humans and dogs belong to?

Scientists have sorted the **animal kingdom** into groups. Here are some of the biggest groups.

Fish
Sharks, goldfish, and salmon are fish.

Insects
Beetles, butterflies, ants, and bees are insects.

Amphibians
Toads, frogs, and newts are amphibians.

Birds
Ducks, eagles, and seagulls are birds.

Reptiles
Lizards, snakes, and turtles are reptiles.

Mammals
Rabbits, seals, and elephants are mammals.

BACKBONES AND VERTEBRATES

You have a row of knobbly bones down the middle of your back. This is your **backbone**. It is also called a spine.

This is part of your skeleton. Your skeleton gives you a shape and keeps you upright.

Animals with a **backbone** are called **vertebrates**.

Backbone

Mammals

Imagine what your body would be like without bones.

Feel your backbone while you move your back. Why do you think that backbones are not just one long bone?

6

Mammals, reptiles, birds, and fish are all **vertebrates**. They all have a **backbone**.

Reptile

Bird

A **backbone** is made up of lots of small bones. A crocodile is very long. Its **backbone** goes from its tail up to its head.

Fish

INVERTEBRATES

Some animals do not have a backbone.
They are called **invertebrates**.
They have soft bodies with no skeleton
inside them.

A scorpion has a skeleton on
the outside of its soft body.

A snail has a hard shell
to protect it.

Snail   **Scorpion**

Many strange-shaped **invertebrates** live underwater, such as squid and jellyfish.

They don't have legs, fins, or flippers. They move around in all kinds of unusual ways.

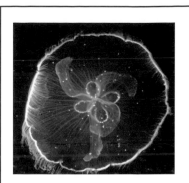

Can you see any bones inside this jellyfish?

Squid

A starfish walks across the rocks using the tiny suckers on its feet.

What animals move in these ways: swim, slither, creep, crawl, scuttle?

Starfish

INSECTS

Insects are invertebrates. They have a body with three parts: the head, thorax, and abdomen.

Insects have a hard case outside their bodies. This case protects them like a suit of armor.

Insects always have six legs and most have wings.

Beetle

Head

Thorax

Abdomen

Why isn't a spider an insect? Count its legs and find out!

All **insects** lay eggs. The eggs hatch into young called larvae. As they grow, the larvae change into the adult **insect**.

Larvae

What flying insects visit flowers?

Take a look at flying insects, but be careful not to disturb them. Bees and wasps can sting!

FISH

Fish live underwater all their lives. They breathe oxygen in the water using gills on each side of their head.

Fish lay eggs that hatch into little fish.

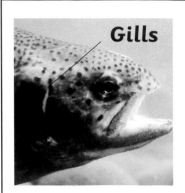

Gills

You can see a fish's gills moving on the side of its head.

Fin

Tail

Eye

Gills

Many **fish** have a long, smooth body. This is a good shape for swimming fast through water.

Fish have strong tails to push them along. Their fins help them to steer.

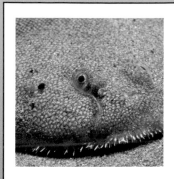

This fish has a flat shape so it can hide in the sand.

Shark

What is similar about the shape of a racing car and a shark?

What else can you think of that has a long, smooth shape?

AMPHIBIANS

Amphibians are animals that have lives in two parts. A frog is an **amphibian.** It spends the first part of its life as a tadpole swimming underwater.

It spends the second part of its life as a frog. It swims in water and hops on land.

Frog

Tadpoles have gills and a tail like a fish.

Newt

Toad

Toads and newts are also **amphibians**.

Adult **amphibians** breathe air, so when they are underwater they must come up to breathe.

They lay their eggs in water so they do not dry out.

If you had very long legs like a frog, how would you move on land?

Can you kick your legs like a frog when you are swimming?

15

REPTILES

Reptiles have dry, scaly, waterproof skins. They use energy from the sun to keep warm.

Lizards and crocodiles bask in the sun to warm up. Some float in the water to cool down.

Lizard

You keep warm from the energy in your food.

16

Tortoises and turtles are **reptiles** with a shell. They move very slowly!

Tortoise

Snake

Snakes are **reptiles** with no legs.

Most snakes move from side to side to slither along the ground.

Reptiles lay their eggs on the ground. Young reptiles look just like adult reptiles.

Old snake skin

As they grow, snakes keep shedding their old skin. What happens to your old skin?

Snake eggs

BIRDS

Birds are the only animals that have feathers. Instead of arms, they have wings.

Birds flap their wings to fly and spread them out to soar through the air.

Not all birds fly. A penguin uses its wings like flippers. They help it to swim.

Duck eggs

Blackbird chicks

Birds lay eggs and sit on them to keep them warm. Inside the eggs, the growing chicks feed on the white and the yolk.

When the chicks hatch, the mother and father **bird** feed them until they can fly away.

Feathers push the air when a bird flaps its wings.

Hold a feather in your hand. Does it feel light or heavy? Why is this important?

Feather

MAMMALS

Most **mammals** have hair on their bodies. They sweat to keep cool. All **mammals** breathe air.

Mammals can look very different. Bats are **mammals** with wings. Whales and seals have flippers.

Some mammals have thick hair on their bodies called fur.

Fur helps to keep this seal warm even in cold, icy places.

Bat

Gibbon

Kangaroo and baby

Nearly all **mammal** babies look like their parents. Only a very few **mammals** lay eggs.

All baby **mammals** drink milk from their mothers. Some grow up in a pouch, like a baby kangaroo.

Enormous blue whales are the largest mammals.

They spend their lives in the ocean but swim to the surface to breathe air.

Do you know what the biggest animal on land is?

LEARNING

A baby elephant **learns** from its mother. It stays with her until it is old enough to look after itself.

Humans **learn** as we grow. We are the only animals that use words to talk and write.

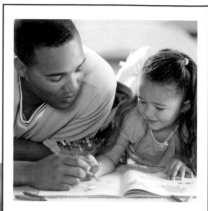

You can learn from books as well as from your parents.

Elephant

What do you see, hear, and smell with? This cow gives you some big clues.

Which parts of your body do you taste or feel with?

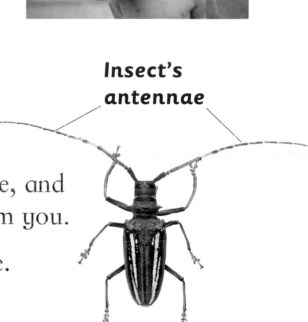

Animals use their senses to **learn** what is going on around them.

Many animals smell, taste, and feel in different ways from you.

Insects use their antennae. Cats use their whiskers. Snakes use their tongues.

Insect's antennae

Snake's tongue

Cat's whiskers

23

NATURE SAFARI

*Look for animals from different
groups in the animal kingdom.*

"I wish we could go on safari and
see lions or tigers!" said Sara.
She shut her book and sighed.

"I'll take you on safari," said Mom.
"Will we see lions or tigers?" asked Owen.
"No, but we'll see all kinds of amazing
animals," said Mom.

They each packed a
knapsack. Owen took a
magnifying glass,
camera, and binoculars.

Sara packed a notebook
and colored pencils.
"I'll take water, apples,
and sandwiches,"
said Mom.

24

"One point for every animal we see," said Sara.
"One point to me then," said Mom, looking at Sara and Owen.

"We're not animals," said Owen.
"Yes, you are," said Mom.
"Humans are animals."

They walked through the forest. "I can't see any animals!" said Owen. "Be patient," said Mom. "Stand very still. Look all around you and listen."

"Most animals are shy," said Sara.

"Even a big deer will run away if it hears, sees, or smells us."

"What are these?" asked Owen.
"Rabbit droppings," said Mom.
"Shush!" said Sara.
"Look in that field."

Owen looked through the binoculars.
"Hundreds of rabbits!" he said. Suddenly, the
rabbits all ran away.

"It's a fox," said Mom.
"He's frightened them away."
Sara wrote rabbits and fox
in her notebook.

"One point to me for
the rabbits. And one
point to Mom for the
fox," she said.

"And a point to me for
spotting the droppings!"
laughed Owen.

"Listen!" said Mom.

They heard a rustling sound above them.

"What's that?" said Sara.

Owen looked through the binoculars. "It's a thrush," he said. "I can see its speckled breast."

"Let me see," said Sara taking the binoculars. "It's feeding a worm to its chicks!" she said.

"I saw the thrush. One point to me!" shouted Owen.

The thrush flew away.

"Shush! Remember to be quiet!" said Sara.

"We've seen mammals and birds so far," said Sara looking at her notebook.

"That pond looks like a good place to see all kinds of animals," said Mom. "But be careful. Don't go too near the edge."

"What's in the water? It looks like spotty jello!" said Sara. "It's frogspawn," said Owen.

A frog plopped into the pond and rings spread out in the water.

Under the water they could see sticklebacks and other small fish.

A cloud of midges buzzed around Owen's head. "They're making my head itch!" he said.

"Put on your hat," said Mom. "That's a point to you. Midges are flying insects!"

"Ooh, look at that beautiful dragonfly!" said Sara. She got out her pencils and sketched the dragonfly before it flew off.

"Watch your feet," said Owen. "Look, there's a slug in the grass. You almost stepped on it!"

Dragonfly

When they got home, Sara checked her notebook. "We saw lots of animal groups!" she said. "And I got the most points!"

"I'll look harder next time," said Owen.

"You can try spotting animals in the yard," said Mom. "Or in the park," said Sara. "There are lots of animals there!"

A fly buzzed past Mom's nose. "There are lots of animals in the house too," she laughed.

WRITE YOUR OWN STORY about a nature walk. Draw pictures of the animals you might see. If you're going on a walk, why not keep a nature notebook like Sara's? Make a chart listing animals in groups.

Mammals	Birds	Insects	Fish	Others
Human	Thrush	Midges	Stickleback	Slug
Rabbit	Owl	Dragonfly		Worm
Fox				Frog

QUIZ

What group of animals do you belong to? Can you name three other animals in this group?

Answers on pages 4 and 20-21

What is the group of animals without **backbones** called? Which member of this group has a shell?

Answer on page 8 9

How do **reptiles** warm up and cool down?

Answer on page 16

Which groups do these belong to?

Milk

Tails and fins

Antennae

Feathers

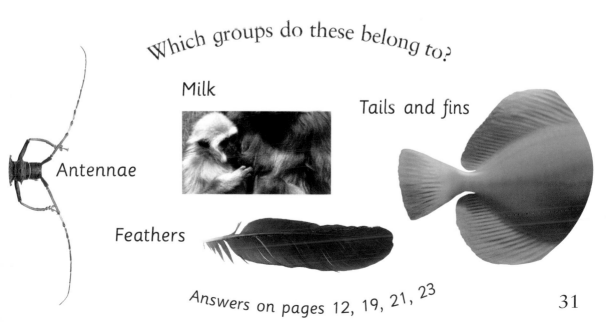

Answers on pages 12, 19, 21, 23

INDEX